KU-312-655

NATURE'S FURY

FOREST FIRE!

Anita Ganeri

FRANKLIN WATTS
LONDON • SYDNEY

First published in 2006 by

Franklin Watts

338 Euston Road

London NW1 3BH

Franklin Watts Australia

Hachette Children's Books

Level 17/207 Kent St, Sydney, NSW 2000

Produced by Arcturus Publishing Limited,

26/27 Bickels Yard, 151–153 Bermondsey Street, London SE1 3HA

J363.379

1738016

© 2006 Arcturus Publishing Limited

Editor: Alex Woolf

Design: www.mindseyedesign.co.uk

Picture credits:

Corbis: 4 (F. Krahmer/zefa), 5 (Jim Sugar), 7 (T. Allofs/zefa), 8 (Aim Patrice), 9 (Dr Vic Bradbury), 10 (Tom Bean), 12 (Reuters), cover and 14 (J. Emilio Flores), 15 (Frank Lane Picture Agency), 16, 18 (Brian A. Vikander), 20 (Parrot Pascal), 21 (Viviane Moos), 23 (Reuters), 24 (Aim Patrice), 25 (Yves Forestier), 26 (John Heseltine), 27 (T. Allofs/zefa), 28 (Dale C. Spartas), 29 (Raymond Gehman).

FLPA: 17 (Michael Quinton/Minden Pictures), 19 (Jim Brandenburg/Minden Pictures).

Mind's Eye Design: 6.

NASA Visible Earth: 11 (Jacques Descloitres, MODIS Land Rapid Response Team at NASA GSFC), 22 (Image by Robert Simmon, based on data from NASA GSFC, MITI, ERSDAC, JAROS, and U.S./Japan ASTER Science Team).

Science Photo Library: 13 (John Reader).

Every attempt has been made to clear copyright. Should there be any inadvertent omission, please apply to the publisher for rectification.

A CIP catalogue record for this book is available from the British Library.

ISBN-10: 07496 6923 3

ISBN-13: 9780749669232

Printed in China

Contents

What is a Forest Fire?

The sight of a fire sweeping furiously through a forest is both frightening and spectacular. Forest fires (also called wildfires) are devastating events. Their intense heat burns leaves and branches to a crisp before making them explode, roaring and crackling, into flames. Giant flames leap hundreds of metres into the air, along with columns of thick, black smoke. In the biggest fires, spinning tornadoes are created by the rapidly rising heat.

▼ *Flames raging through a coniferous forest in the Yosemite National Park in California, USA.*

A fiery path

Even the biggest forest fire starts as a tiny spark. If the vegetation is dry enough, the spark quickly grows into an inferno. Flames spread in all directions, burning everything in

their path. They damage and kill trees, incinerate plants on the forest floor, and even kill roots under the ground. Buildings in the way are also burned. Any unfortunate people or animals who become trapped between the fast-moving flames may be killed by smoke. When the flames are gone, a charred, smoking wasteland is left behind. Firefighters do not attempt to put out intense forest fires. Instead they try to stop the fires from spreading and allow the flames to burn themselves out.

Where and why?

Forest fires happen in places where hot summer weather dries out dense vegetation. They happen more often during droughts. The dry vegetation catches light very easily, allowing the fire to spread rapidly. Fire affects both coniferous forests and deciduous forests. It can also burn across grasslands, scrub and heather moorlands. Most forest fires are started accidentally by people, but some are started naturally by lightning.

▲ *Scientists cutting a slice from a giant sequoia tree. The tree rings will tell them when forest fires happened in the past.*

A NATURAL CYCLE

Lightning has been starting forest fires throughout history. Layers of charcoal in rocks tell us that there were devastating fires millions of years ago. Blackened tree rings in very old trees show that natural forest fires are regular events in some places. Although forest fires can be very damaging, they are not always bad news. Fire clears out old trees and allows new ones to grow. There is a natural cycle of fire and regrowth. In fact, some species of trees could not survive without regular fires.

What is a Fire?

Before we can investigate how forest fires burn and how firefighters combat them, we need to understand what exactly fire is. A fire is made up of glowing, red-hot material and often flames. These give off heat and normally produce smoke. Fire happens when a material burns. Burning is a chemical reaction between a material and oxygen, which is one of the gases in the air. Burning is also called combustion.

The fire triangle

A fire must have three things to keep burning. They are fuel, heat and oxygen. These three things make up the 'fire triangle'. A fuel is any material that burns – not just the fuels we use for heating, in cars, and so on. You can find out about the fuels in forest fires on pages 12–13. Fuel must be heated before it will burn and this heat must be provided for a fire to start. Once a fire is burning, however, it produces its own heat, and so it can carry on burning. Oxygen comes from the air, so a fire needs a supply of air.

▼ *This diagram is known as the fire triangle. The elements on all three sides must be there for the fire to continue burning.*

Flames and smoke

Plant matter, such as wood and leaves, is made up of several substances, including cellulose and lignin. When plant matter is heated, these substances begin to break up. Some flammable gases are given off. These burn in the air, giving off heat and light, which we see as flames. The material that remains is mostly carbon. Carbon glows red as it burns. Some tiny bits of unburned carbon are carried into the air. These mix with the air to form smoke. Water from the plant material boils in the heat, making steam that rises with the smoke.

◀ *A close-up of the intense heat in a fire. The tree bark is glowing as the carbon in it burns.*

STOPPING FIRE

If you remove one of the three sides of the fire triangle (fuel, heat or oxygen), the fire cannot keep burning. So if the fuel runs out, the heat is taken away or the oxygen supply is cut off, the fire goes out. These are the basic ways of fighting fire. Firefighters can stop a fire by taking away fuel, cooling it with water or smothering it with foam.

How Forest Fires Start

Two conditions are needed for a forest fire to start. Firstly, the forest fuel (the trees, other plants and dead matter on the forest floor) must be dry. Secondly, there must a source of heat to ignite the fuel and start the fire.

Where fires happen

Forest fires happen most regularly in parts of the world where winters are cool and wet and summers are hot and dry. This sort of climate provides good growing conditions for trees and other plants, so there is plenty of vegetation around. But in the summer the vegetation can dry out. Two of the world's forest fire hotspots are the west of North

▲ *Firefighters work to control a fire in the Castellet area of southern France. The fires were a result of drought in 2001.*

CASE STUDY

Fire in France

Summers in the south of France are very hot and very dry. These conditions dry out the forests. Hundreds of fires start every year, and major fires burn every six years or so. The fires are made worse by the mistral, a strong north-westerly wind that often blows through the valleys during the summer. This fans the flames, allowing the fires to spread dangerously fast.

America and south-east Australia, where there are thousands of fires every year. However, in severe droughts fires can even rage in tropical rainforests, where conditions are normally too wet for fires to start.

The fire season

Forest fires normally burn during the dry, summer months, but they can also burn in spring and autumn. The period of the year when fires are most likely is called the fire season. Drought makes fires far more likely because the lack of rain leaves the vegetation very dry. Drought happens if seasonal rains fail to arrive, or if there is low rainfall for months on end.

What ignites fires?

Fires are either started by natural events or by people, either accidentally or deliberately. By far the most common natural fire starter is lightning. Lightning hits the Earth about 100,000 times every day. It is the major cause of fire in remote areas. Fires are occasionally started by volcanic eruptions. Another cause is the build-up of heat from rotting vegetation on the forest floor, known as spontaneous combustion.

▲ *When lightning strikes a tree, a huge electric current flows through the tree. This heats the tree very quickly, which can make it ignite.*

Human-made Forest Fires

In the USA, four out of five forest fires are started by people. In Australia the figure is nine out of ten. Most are caused accidentally, but some are started deliberately, either for land management or to reduce fire risk (see pages 28–29).

Accidental fires

Forest fires are started accidentally in many ways. A common cause is campfires that get out of control or that are not put out properly. Discarded matches and cigarette butts, and domestic rubbish fires also start fires. Sparks from trains and logging machines can ignite fires if they fall into very dry litter on the forest floor.

▼ *Campfires are a major cause of forest fires. They must be carefully controlled to stop fire spreading to nearby vegetation.*

Fire for land management

It is thought that humans discovered how to make fire more than 60,000 years ago. People soon learned to use fire to their advantage, and for thousands of years fire has been used to clear vegetation to make space to grow crops, graze animals and make hunting easier. One of the major causes of forest fires today is slash-and-burn land clearance (also called shift cultivation). This is practised in rainforests, such as the Amazon rainforest, to clear land for crops and cattle. During a drought, these fires can easily get out of control, causing major damage.

Deliberate fires

A surprising number of forest fires are started deliberately for no real reason. In the USA, about one in four human-made fires is lit by vandals. Some are lit for revenge, perhaps to try to burn down property close to the forest. People also light them simply for the thrill of seeing a fire.

▲ *Each red dot here is a forest fire on the island of Borneo in Indonesia, seen in 2002. Most were caused by slash-and-burn fires getting out of control.*

CASE STUDY

Indonesian fires, 1997

The tropical forests of Indonesia are being cleared by slash-and-burn farmers and also by companies to make space to grow trees for paper-making and palm oil. In 1997, the forests were very dry because seasonal rains had failed to arrive, and many fires got out of control. Some burned for months before being extinguished by rain. Smoke from the fires affected many cities in Malaysia, Indonesia and Singapore, and millions of people were treated for breathing problems.

How Forest Fires Spread

▼ *A forest fire on Cyprus. The fire spread quickly up the mountain slopes, fanned by high winds.*

Heat produced by a fire moves by convection (hot air currents) and radiation (heat rays). This makes the surrounding fuel hot enough to catch fire. The fuel burns too, first making flames and then smouldering, until the fuel is used up. In this way, a line of flames called a flame front moves through the forest, spreading in every direction from the source of the fire.

Spreading factors

The intensity of a fire and the speed of a flame front depend on several factors. Wind is very important. Wind brings fresh supplies of air to a fire, fanning the flames and causing a fire to burn more quickly. Wind also affects the direction in which a fire burns. A flame front moves more quickly in the direction of the wind and more slowly against the wind. Slope affects a fire, too. Fire burns more quickly uphill because heat from a fire rises into the vegetation further up the slope. Due to these factors, a fire's flame front moves at different speeds in different directions.

Forest fire fuel

The material that burns in a forest fire is known as fuel. A forest can contain just a couple of types of fuel, or dozens of different fuels. The needles, leaves and branches of trees are not the only fuel. Small trees, shrubs and grasses on the forest floor also burn, as do fallen leaves and needles (known as litter), and fallen branches. Even rotting leaves and logs beneath the forest floor burn, and so do roots under the ground. The more fuel there is, and the drier the conditions, the more intense the fire. The type of fuel affects the intensity of a fire. For example, deciduous trees burn more slowly than conifers. Some vegetation, such as eucalyptus trees, burns more rapidly because it contains flammable oils.

▲ *In this grassland fire the fuel is dry grass. The grass burns quickly, allowing the fire to spread rapidly.*

FIRE SPEED

The speed at which a flame front moves depends on the wind, the landscape and the fuel available. In a deciduous woodland, in calm conditions, fire creeps slowly, perhaps at only 0.5 kilometres per hour (about 15 centimetres per second). But in windy conditions, fire can spread across dry grasslands at 8 kilometres per hour, which is faster than walking pace.

Types of Forest Fire

Firefighters classify fires by the way they spread through a forest. They divide the forest horizontally into three layers. The crown is the top layer, made up of the branches, needles and leaves of mature trees. The surface layer is the forest floor. The ground layer is under the surface.

Crown, surface and ground fires

Crown fires burn in the crown. They spread through the treetops, with flames leaping from one tree to the next. They tend to occur during strong winds and spread quickly, leaving the forest floor below untouched. Crown fires happen in thick conifer forests and are the fiercest forest fires.

Surface fires burn on the forest floor, through young trees, shrubs and grasses. They also burn fresh, dry litter that has

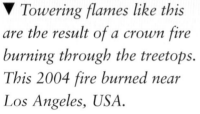

▼ *Towering flames like this are the result of a crown fire burning through the treetops. This 2004 fire burned near Los Angeles, USA.*

fallen from the trees, dead logs and branches. Surface fires normally leave the crown above untouched, unless wind carries the flames upwards. Most forest fires are surface fires.

Ground fires burn material in the ground, under the surface. They do not burn with flames, but smoulder, making little smoke. They burn slowly through decaying needles and leaves, and the roots of plants, often unseen.

Blow-ups and fire devils

In thick conifer forests, where there is a plentiful supply of dry fuel, forest fires can burn very intensely. Needles dry out instantly and burn violently. A column of hot air rises from the fire, pulling fresh air in from the sides, which fans the flames. Temperatures can reach more than 1,000 degrees centigrade, and flames leap hundreds of metres upwards. These terrifying fires are known as blow-ups. The swirling air currents sometimes cause whirlwinds or mini-tornadoes, known as fire devils.

▲ *Fire has damaged this forest of eucalyptus trees in Portugal. It has spread along the surface and through the crowns.*

CASE STUDY

Australian bush fires

South-east Australia is one of the world's forest fire hotspots. The summers are very hot and dry, and there is little rain in winter. The forests contain many eucalyptus trees, which burn easily. In early 1983, a ten-month drought was followed by strong winds. Hundreds of fires started when trees blew into power lines. They spread ferociously. Flames measuring 375 metres high were seen and 350,000 hectares of land were burned, along with 2,300 houses. Seventy-one people died.

Fire and the Landscape

How a fire affects the forest trees depends on the type of fire and the trees themselves. A surface fire kills young trees with branches and leaves close to the ground. Older, taller trees, with bare lower trunks and crowns high up, normally survive surface fires because their thick bark protects the delicate cambium (growing layer) underneath. However, even slight bark damage can let in harmful diseases and insects. Intense crown fires tend to kill older, larger trees, but these trees can still lose up to a third of their crowns and survive. Ground fires can kill young and old trees by damaging their roots.

▼ *The charred remains of a forest after a fire. Every tree has been damaged by the intense heat, but some trees may still be alive.*

Changes to soil

Intense heat destroys some of the nutrients in forest soil. If the layer of decaying vegetation is burned, the micro-organisms that recycle nutrients are also killed. On the positive side, ash from the burned plants mixes with the soil, and this ash contains nutrients such as potassium, magnesium and calcium.

Where plant roots are killed and decaying vegetation is burned, the soil has nothing to protect it from erosion. Heavy rain washes it away easily, especially on sloping ground. This leaves no soil for new plants to grow in. The rain also washes ash into streams and rivers.

Effects on animals

Many large animals are able to survive forest fires by running, and birds can fly away. Animals that live in underground burrows, such as rodents, survive because the soil protects them from the heat, but they may still be harmed by the heat from ground fires. However, many small animals, such as insects, cannot escape. Larger animals that do die are killed by smoke rather than flames. Animal habitats are also destroyed by fire, as are nests and eggs.

▲ *An elk in the Yellowstone National Park, USA, in 1988. In the background is smoke from giant forest fires. The elk is in more danger from the smoke than from the fire.*

CASE STUDY

Yellowstone National Park, 1988

In the summer of 1988, a series of fires devastated parts of Yellowstone National Park in north-western USA. The intensity of the fires was caused by a lack of rain and snow over the previous months. Hundreds of fires were set off by lightning. Forest officials allowed some of the fires to burn, but the fires quickly grew out of control. Over the summer months, 320,000 hectares (the same area as 150,000 football pitches) of forest were burned. Thousands of animals died, including 250 elks.

Forest Recovery

The blackened, smouldering landscape left behind by a forest fire appears lifeless. It is hard to believe that any plant or animal could live there again. But no matter how devastating a fire is, the forest always recovers eventually. A few months after the fire, green shoots begin to rise from the soil. Plants and animals gradually return, and within ten to twenty years all traces of the fire are gone. Forest fires have been raging on Earth for millions of years, and forests have always recovered naturally.

Succession

The order in which different plants return to a scorched landscape is called succession. Ash from the fire supplies nutrients to plants, so growth is often rapid. Small plants such as weeds and grasses return first. These are known as

▼ *Grasses growing on the forest floor in Montana, USA, after a fire in 1988. Many trees are still charred from the flames.*

pioneer plants. Some grow from seeds left in the soil. Others spread from the surrounding, unburned forest. Next come shrubs, and then trees. Plants that survive the fire also begin to grow again. Light-loving plants often thrive until the recovering trees begin to block out the light again. Animals that live on the newly growing plants return to the forest before larger, predatory animals.

Adapting to fire

Some plants are well adapted to survive the heat of forest fires. For example, the giant sequoia has tough, thick bark, deep roots and branches that are out of reach of surface fires. The aspen can grow new shoots from any of its roots that remain undamaged. Some plants even take advantage of fire to reproduce. Some plant seeds lie dormant in the soil, perhaps for many decades, until the heat of a fire opens them up.

▲ *This is a seedling of a type of pine tree called a jack pine. It has grown after its cone was opened by the heat of a forest fire.*

FIRE PINES

A few species of pine trees rely on fire to reproduce. They are known as fire pines and they are found in forests where fire is a regular event. Their cones are held together by sticky resin. The resin melts in the heat of a fire, releasing the seeds. Without fire, the species would die out.

Forest Fires and People

▼ *A forest fire threatens a house near Marseilles in France. The house is at great risk because it is surrounded by trees.*

Forest fires are a serious danger to people. Although smoke gives plenty of warning of approaching flames and most fires can be outrun, forest workers, campers and walkers are regularly killed in forest fires. They often become confused in the smoke, heat and noise and get trapped between two flame fronts. They are killed by the dense smoke. Only forest fires in very remote areas do not affect people.

Building damage

Thousands of homes and even whole towns are built close to forests that are prone to fires. When a fire occurs, houses and other buildings are ignited by the heat from nearby burning trees, or by flying embers landing on them. Many houses in these areas are built from wood and so they burn very quickly.

The local infrastructure is also often affected. Roads and railways are closed due to falling trees and smoke. Communication and power lines are damaged and have to be repaired. After a serious fire, the land around buildings can suffer erosion and sometimes mudslides. The soil can be stabilized by covering it with mats and fast-growing plants.

Economic damage

Timber companies plant millions of conifer trees in vast plantations, mostly in countries in the northern hemisphere. The wood from the fully grown trees is used for construction and as a source of wood pulp for paper making. Fires are common in these plantations, particularly during hot, dry summers. Fire spreads through the densely packed trees quickly. Fire damage to plantations is extremely costly. Fire kills young trees that would have provided timber in the future, and new trees have to be planted to replace them. Forest fires are also damaging to tourist and leisure businesses because camping, walking and fishing are disrupted.

▲ The smoke from forest fires can affect people's health. These people in the city of Kuala Lumpur, Malaysia, are wearing masks against smoke from forest fires in Indonesia.

CASE STUDY

Cedar Fire, 2003

The Cedar Fire was one of the most devastating fires in Californian history. It was one of a series of fires in southern California in October 2003. Started accidentally by hunters, the Cedar Fire spread rapidly through the thick scrub, driven by hot, dry winds. More than 100,000 hectares of land were burned and more than 2,000 homes, buildings and bridges were destroyed around San Diego. Fourteen people died, most as they tried to escape the flames in their cars.

Fighting Forest Fires

The first stage in fighting a forest fire is to detect that the fire has started. If this is done early, the fire can be stopped before it grows. If a fire has become established, senior firefighters make a plan of attack. They use information about the fuel in the forest, the weather and the terrain to decide how to tackle the fire. Firefighters don't always try to put out forest fires. They sometimes leave them to burn themselves out, providing they are sure that no people or properties are at risk.

Fire detection

At times of high fire risk, people are always on the lookout for telltale smoke from forest fires. In some places there are manned fire-watch stations on hilltops. In others, rangers patrol the forest in vehicles or in aircraft. If smoke is spotted, the next step is to pinpoint the exact location of the fire.

▶ *A fire in Idaho, USA, seen from space. At the height of the fire, 1787 people, 16 helicopters, 47 fire engines, and 20 bulldozers were fighting it.*

This is not easy in cases where there is lots of smoke, so an aircraft carrying a heat-sensing infrared scanner flies over the area. Once the fire has been pinpointed, maps can be drawn for the fire-control team. Now firefighters move into position by foot, truck and aircraft.

Direct and indirect attack

Firefighters attack a fire directly or indirectly, or sometimes with both methods. Direct firefighting is used on small fires before they spread. Firefighters try to put the fire out by hosing it with water, covering it with earth or ash, raking away the fuel or hitting it with beaters.

Indirect firefighting is used on intense fires. Firefighters do not try to put out the flames, but try to stop the fire spreading. They clear sections of forest ahead of the flame front, creating firebreaks that the fire cannot cross. They light fires called backfires that burn towards the flame front, using up the fuel. They also try to slow the fire's spread with water and fire retardants (see page 25). These are sprayed onto vegetation ahead of the flame front.

▲ *Firefighters and soldiers build a firebreak in the Payette National Forest in Idaho, USA. The firebreak is designed to stop the fire from spreading.*

FIREBREAKS

A firebreak (or fire line) is a wide corridor through the forest. Firefighters make a firebreak by cutting down trees, stripping away other vegetation, scraping away litter and digging out roots. They use hand tools and bulldozers. Roads, railway lines, rivers and lakes act as natural firebreaks.

Firefighting Equipment

Fighting a forest fire is very different from fighting a house fire. Forest firefighters must work over a huge area. They must make firebreaks as well as trying to control flames. Forest firefighters use a wide range of specialist equipment, from simple hand tools to giant aircraft.

▼ A French firefighter sprays water onto a surface fire. The water cools the fire, preventing more fuel from igniting.

Hand tools

Firefighters use rakes for clearing burning material, shovels for digging, beaters to beat down flames and chainsaws for cutting down trees. American firefighters also use a tool called a pulaski, which is like an axe and hoe combined. They use it for chopping away branches and for scraping away vegetation and litter. The pulaski was invented in 1913 by park ranger Edward Pulaski.

Firefighters also carry personal safety equipment and wear fireproof suits and helmets. They use portable, heat-resistant shelters that are like tents with an aluminium covering. These shelters protect firefighters from temperatures of up to 315 degrees centigrade.

Firefighting machinery

All-wheel-drive fire trucks carry firefighters and equipment, including long hoses and water pumps, into the forest. Some have on-board water tanks; others pull tanker trailers. Bulldozers are used to uproot trees and clear earth to make firebreaks. Aircraft drop firefighters and equipment into the fire zone, help to keep track of the fire and assist in rescuing people. Aircraft can also scoop up water from lakes and drop it into the flames. Fixed-wing aircraft can carry several tonnes of water. Fire retardants may be mixed with the water. These are chemicals that coat vegetation and stop it burning so intensely.

◄ A firefighting aircraft drops fire retardant onto flames in the south of France. Dropping the chemicals in the right place is a skilled job.

 FIRE JUMPERS

In very remote areas it would take many hours for trucks to reach a fire. So the initial attack on the fire is made by firefighters called fire jumpers (or smoke jumpers). They parachute into the forest carrying all the equipment they need, plus food, water and first-aid equipment. Fire jumpers can often reach a fire in its early stages before it has a chance to spread.

Fire Warnings and Protection

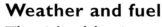

▼ *These are fire beaters, used to beat out flames. They are positioned in areas of high fire risk.*

During the fire season, the authorities in forest fire hotspots constantly monitor forests to calculate the chances of major fires occurring. When the risk is high, firefighters can be kept on standby and the public can be alerted to the danger.

Weather and fuel

The risk of fire increases as forest vegetation dries out over the summer. The weather is a guide to how dry the fuel will be, so temperature, rainfall and humidity are constantly recorded. During the fire season, portable weather stations are installed deep in forests to send back weather data. Forest rangers also analyse the dryness and quantity of fuel. Lightning starts many forest fires, and if electrical storms are forecast, then fires are more likely. Monitoring lightning strikes is helpful for predicting where fires could start. This monitoring is done by ground-based automatic lightning detection systems.

Predicting how a fire will spread

Once a fire has started, experts try to predict how it will spread. This helps firefighters as well as allowing the authorities to put out warnings and organize evacuations. Weather data and information about fuel and terrain are entered into a computer model, which draws a map showing the risks to different areas.

Fire protection

If a forest fire is surrounding a human settlement, people must protect themselves and their homes as best they can. Firefighters advise them to wear cotton or wool clothes, gloves, goggles and a helmet. They should collect as much water in containers as possible, along with wet blankets and rugs for beating out flames. As the fire passes, they should stay indoors and then try to put out any fires that have started in the house. Houses in or near forests have a better chance of survival if they are built with fire-resistant materials, such as brick, and with a large clearing around them.

FIRE DANGER
LOW
TODAY!
PREVENT WILDFIRES

▲ *A fire danger sign in Joshua Tree National Park, USA. A low risk probably means that there has been rain recently.*

FIRE DANGER RATING SYSTEMS

Several countries, including the USA, Canada and Australia, operate a fire danger rating system. This is a scale that tells the public the risk of forest fires starting in their area. The danger rating is available on the Internet or by phone. The rating is also displayed on noticeboards to deter people from entering forests at times of high risk. The US system, the National Fire Danger Rating System (NFDRS), has five levels: low (shown on maps in dark green); moderate (light green or blue); high (yellow); very high (orange); and extreme (red).

Preventing Forest Fires

▲ *A forester lighting a fire in a plantation to burn away dead vegetation. This helps to prevent fires damaging the valuable wood.*

Forest fire experts often say that the best way of fighting a forest fire is to stop it from starting in the first place. We cannot stop lightning from igniting fires, but we can try to prevent fires from starting accidentally, especially during the fire season.

Education programmes

Fire-risk education programmes are designed to reduce the frequency of forest fires that are started accidentally. Programmes are composed of classroom visits and advertising campaigns. Noticeboards, posters and road signs in forests inform visitors of the dos and don'ts of fire prevention, such as putting out cigarettes properly and taking care with camping stoves.

Campfire control

Campfires are a major cause of forest fires. They either spread to surrounding vegetation and get out of control or are not put out properly and ignite again after campers have left. Fire prevention advice for campers includes:

- Don't light a fire at all in times of high fire risk.
- Scrape away needles and leaf litter to make a patch of bare soil or rock at least two metres across.

- Light only a small fire.
- Dip dead matches in water to make sure they are out.
- Watch the fire all the time to make sure it is under control.
- Before leaving camp, drown the fire with water and soak the ground around it.

Forest management

Forest fires can also be prevented by careful forest management. For example, when the risk of fires is high, the authorities can close the forests to the public and suspend logging.

Forest managers can reduce the intensity of forest fires by occasionally setting light to forests on purpose. These fires are called prescribed fires. They burn away litter and vegetation on the forest floor, stopping a build-up of fuel that could lead to a catastrophic fire in the future. Prescribed fires must be carefully planned so that they cannot spread.

▲ *A child learns about fire fighting at a forest visitor centre in California, USA. The fire-education mascot, Smokey Bear, is watching in the background.*

SMOKEY BEAR

The cartoon character Smokey Bear is the mascot of the American forest fire education programme for young children. The US Forest Service has been running the programme since 1944. Records show that the area of forest burned each year in the early 21st century is less than a quarter of that burned before the campaign began.

TEN OF THE DEADLIEST FOREST FIRES

WHEN	WHERE	CASUALTIES
1871	Peshtigo, Wisconsin, USA	1,200 to 2,000
1949	Cloquet, Minnesota / Wisconsin, USA	400 to 500
1894	Hinckley, Minnesota, USA	418
1881	Thumb, Michigan, USA	282
1987	North-east China	212
1825	Miramichi, New Brunswick, USA	160
1939	Victoria, Australia	76
1983	Victoria / South Australia	71
1967	Hobart, Australia	62
2003	Portugal	18

GLOSSARY

carbon A chemical element that is the main building block of all animals and plants.

cellulose A natural substance that makes up the cell walls of plants. Cellulose is also used as a fibre in textiles.

combustion A chemical reaction in which a substance combines with oxygen in the air. Another word for burning.

conifer A tree that has thin needles rather than leaves, and releases seeds from cones.

convection A movement of heat by air currents.

deciduous Describes a tree that loses its leaves every year.

dormant Inactive, but not dead.

drought A period of time when there is little or no rainfall.

erosion The wearing away of rock and soil by natural forces, such as running water.

flammable Describes a material that burns easily.

humidity A measure of the amount of water vapour in the atmosphere.

incinerate Burn until only ash is left.

inferno An intense fire producing huge amounts of heat.

infrared scanner A device that detects infrared (heat) radiation.

infrastructure Structures for transport, power supply and communications, such as roads, railways, bridges, water supply pipes and electricity pylons.

lignin A natural substance that strengthens the parts of plants.

micro-organism An animal or plant that is so small that it can only be seen through a microscope. Bacteria are micro-organisms.

nutrient A substance needed by plants and animals to live and grow.

oxygen A chemical element that is found as a gas in the atmosphere.

radiation A form of energy that travels in the form of rays or waves, such as heat, light and radio waves.

slash-and-burn land clearance Clearing land for crops or grazing by cutting down and burning forest.

tornado A spinning column of air that forms under a thunder cloud.

FURTHER INFORMATION

Books
The Atlas of the World's Worst Natural Disasters by Lesley Newson (Dorling Kindersley, 1998).

Fire and Flood by Nicola Barber (Ticktock Publishing, 1999).

Websites
www.fs.fed.us/fire/
The wildfire section of the US Forest Service website.

www.smokeybear.com
The website of the Smokey Bear anti-fire education programme.

www.fs.fed.us/land/wfas/nfdr_adjective.html
A list of the US fire danger ratings.

www.fs.fed.us/fire/people/smokejumpers
All about smoke jumpers.

www.fs.fed.us/land/wfas/fd_class.gif
An up-to-date fire-danger map for the USA.

http://earthobservatory.nasa.gov/NaturalHazards
Select 'Fire' for satellite images of the latest forest fires.

INDEX

Page numbers in **bold** refer to illustrations.